Nuffink in Particular

Part Three

A collection of poems and sketches

by

Ted Roche

ISBN: 978-1-7398885-0-3

Published in the UK by:

Louannvee Publishing
https://www.louannveepublishing.co.uk

For

Davina

Acknowledgements

I should like to thank my publisher Louannvee and in particular Nettie for all her help, expertise and enthusiasm in producing the book and a big thank you to members of my U3A poetry group for their support and encouragement.

CONTENTS

FAMILY

A Few Memory Fragments

RELATIONSHIPS

Cynical Snippets

PEOPLE

CONTENTS

FRIENDS

TRAVEL

SOCIAL ISSUES

CONTENTS

NATURE

MISCELLANEOUS

COVID POEMS AFTER AUGUST 2020

Preface

Following the publication of *Nuffink in Particular Parts One and Two* and the supportive and kind comments, from readers, I now move on to offer my latest book entitled *Nuffink in Particular Part Three.* Much of this collection was in fact completed over two years ago but was side tracked and mothballed by the Covid Pandemic, which in turn prompted the publication of *Somefink in Particular* which traced, again in poems, sketches and anecdotes, the first six months of the epidemic. Unlike the first two books, where the content was presented in no strict order I have, in this edition, attempted to group the offerings under various themes and topics.

Visit https://www.louannveepublishing.co.uk to discover more about Ted Roche and his published works:

Nuffink in Particular Part One

Nuffink in Particular Part Two

Nuffink in Particular Part Three

Somefink in Particular

FAMILY

"Life begins and ends with family and we fill the space between"

A Few Memory Fragments

Cobden Street Poplar 1950's

Sundays taken to grandparents in Cobden Street E14
A small terraced house. Front step scrubbed,
as were most.
Front door always open and knocker polished,
as were most.

Into the hallway with 'Parlour' on the left.
Sombre and dark. Piano. Clock on mantelpiece.
Pigeon trophies and floral vase on chest-of-draws.
Room rarely used. 'Only for best'
Down the hallway another living room on left.
Victorian furniture. More used and on the
right, stairs to upper floor. Never went upstairs.
Down two or three steps to engine room, 'The Kitchen'
Where rain or shine, winter or summer everyone
spent most of the time.
There were seven children but now only two living at
home: Uncle John, dad's younger brother and Aunt Vera,
youngest of the seven.
A 'Kitchener' on the right with grandad's Windsor chair
close by. He sat there most of the time after a stroke.
Nan: a short, plump, homely and kind lady. Always gave
me bread and jam.
A table on the left and behind it a window to the
outside. Many old Robinson's 'golly labels' stuck on
window. Nothing to do with 'racism'. Just decoration.

Through the kitchen and into the 'Scullery' with
large copper sink and door into the yard.
Tomato plants on left and pigeon lofts on right

and bottom. Lofts took up seventy percent of space.
Close to the back door the outside loo. The only loo.
A single wooden bench with a hole in the middle
and squares of newspaper hanging from a piece of string.
Not a place to stay long, especially in the winter.

Next door lived 'Old Laura'.
Thin, lined face, hair in a bun. Always wore plimsolls.
Had been a 'Knocker up' i.e. used a long pole to knock on
peoples windows to wake them for work in the early hours.

Growing Up

As I grew up
religion was poured over me.
Not with fire and brimstone
or by some fascist dressed as a priest
but by love, parental love,
parental certainty, more precisely,
a mother's certainty.

As I grew up,
it was natural seduction,
acquiescence by routine.
A tight fitting sweater of morality
folded around those years,
so snug, so cosy,
a blanket of security.

With adolescence comes exposure.
Tight fitting morality itches.
Comforts become irksome.
One starts to pull and struggle,
stretch and fight.
Instincts incarcerated scream to be free.

And so it's cast off.
A new, more fashionable
sweater of 'mores' pulled over.
Liberation embraced.
Or was it?
Was it only masked freedom?
Illusion gymnastics?

As the years pass
the imprint is realised.
Involuntarily displayed
in reaction and response.

Feelings from the pit
that can't be scourged.
Socialisation.

Age should bring certainty
not more confusion.
Age should bring peace
not fear of death.

One remembers now
that snug and cosy
blanket of security.

Definition

There's no such thing as a
lapsed catholic; just someone
who stopped going to church.

Old Holiday Photos

So many lives all boxed in a Brownie
Out they all tumble in Ventnor or Hove
Laughing in Swanage, scowling at Walton,
Beach huts and tummies, a crab on the toe.

They breathe for a while, at least while we're looking,
They live in our minds, our eyes give them blood,
They're swimming or digging or muffled from cold,
Did the sun always shine? Can't quite remember.

A sister still pouting. "You look like a cod"
Her teenage years passing but not fast enough,
She sees without looking the boys hanging round,
She poses all day, all sophisticated day.

Hold every second of sand pies and castles,
Climbing dad's tummy we stop for a rest,
There's a dog sniffing round, "Watch out for your sandwich"
Too late, "Get away," "He's peed on the chair"!

The sun says we're swimming; Aunt Ellie too,
The water's inviting but "Dad it's so cold"
Now it's the breast stroke, the crawl and the splash,
It's diving and fighting, "He hit me first"!

Let's look at another from out of the pile.
The sister, her friend, my brother and me,
The aunt and the uncle, our mum and dad,
All placed in a shelter like dolls in a row.
"Mum when are we gonna eat, I'm hungry"?

We're outside the digs with landlady buxom,
Did know her name but not any more,
She lived near the sea but never went down there,
Treacle of pudding sticks in the mind.

Go back in the dark now people I loved,
You live just through me but now that's enough,
For a while I felt happy but now that has changed,
I can't bring you back and that makes me sad.

Generations

My parents generation, after the war,
rarely touched, rarely hugged, rarely kissed,
except when timetabled for weddings or funerals,
rarely said “I love you,” “Can't live without you,”
except when registered for passion or grief,
in private but sometimes not even then.

And yet there was warmth, more masked,
not overt, more clandestine but there most obviously.
Words not said, words in hiding, feelings concealed
but there most obviously in daily routine.

My parents were not repressed, cold or frigid
They hugged through sandwiches in my dad's briefcase
kissed through the handles of mum's shopping bag
Said 'I love you' via meat pie and jam roly-poly
They were touching all the time.

So now it's overt routine;
'Love you' 'Love me' 'Love you babe'
'Give me a hug' 'Give me a kiss'
'Love you forever' 'Can't live without you'
''Turned out nice again'
'Oh, that could be the postman'!

Does the equation 'more overt' = 'more healthy, less
repressed' or in substance,
has love never really changed?

A Pauper

I've just heard that my grandfather x three
was declared a pauper in 1817!!
The overseer's records show it
and there it is in black and white!

But surely not!
He was a respectable man.
A man with a trade, a carpenter,
long time married, father of seven.
Surely a respectable man!

Now lying in bed, through half closed eyes,
I'm resolved to tackle him on the matter.
The family history reputation depends on it.

His reply, although hesitant, is unequivocal.
A victim of the depression that followed the
Napoleonic wars. Like so many others
a good man fallen on hard times.
OK fair enough. Explanation given.

But wait...
Now he says he also had a slipped disc
so painful he couldn't move; let alone work.
And the man from 'the parish'
had an 'attitude problem' and was very rude.
Called him 'a lazy good for nothing' and was
determined to get him on the 'paupers register'.
That's what he says!

Now I'm beginning to question his whole account
And when I suggest that he was always a poor husband,
a drinker, womaniser and general waste of space
methinks he protests too much!

In the end, the truth is hard to come by
and I suppose one just has to admit,
two hundred year old people can be very unreliable.

In the Early Hours. 1968

In the early hours of a cold Paddington November morning
we sat together in a job-lot, cream and brown, painted corridor
on functional, non de-script, wooden, hospital benches
and waited, without conversation, for my father to die.

He was in an adjacent room
and we sat listening, without comment, to his loud
but laboured, intermittent, staccato attempts to breath.
My mothers hand gripping mine
as the clock moved inevitably, second by irresistible second
towards the epilogue of his contribution.

He was a good man; everybody said that.
A kind, considerate man; everybody said that,
so the incidence of a long, protracted, painful illness
did not somehow seem to conform to any considered
notion of justice or fair play; everybody said that.

Suddenly, after an hour or so, the note changed to a
guttural, rasping, choking sound which spilled out
and echoed into the cream and brown corridor.
My mothers grip becoming vice like.

As we left the hospital; grey dawn emerging,
a grief tempered by the relief of conclusion
signalled my father moving on and of course
subsequently, our moving on.

Sister

When I last saw you I was shocked.
Shocked to see a shell. A wizened shell
wrapped over life.
Shocked to see that life
retreating, ebbing, sliding away
so fast.

Such a pretty girl, such a beautiful woman.
The thief of time never laid a glove on you.
Never made a dent.
You ignored him, skipped round him,
mocked him even
until now.

But as I sat and looked and held your hand
you drifted back to us.
Just for a while, not for long,
just a few minutes.
And as I joked, you smiled, you spoke
and then it was you
no longer a shell,
a beautiful sister
returned.

RELATIONSHIPS

"Relationships can be seen as a series of chances that can twist and turn and change direction with a breath of wind"

Attraction

For Her:
There must be some attraction.
Maybe not strong at first but something
A smile, a look, a gesture, the voice, something

- Only later -

With smelly socks, smelly armpits and smelly pants
the veil thins.

- And later still -

With a beer belly, burping and farting
it disappears altogether.

For Him:
There must be a good figure and shapely bottom

- And later -

There must be a good figure and shapely bottom

- And later still -

There must be the illusion of a good figure and
shapely bottom.

Carnal Relations

Before:
He said: Look before we start it's best to tell you I don't
like any rough stuff; being biffed around or
anything!
She said: OK so what have you got in mind?
He said: Well, I think it might be best if I just lay here
quietly and leave you to get on with it!!

After:
She said: Thanks Dave, despite everything,
that was very nice.
He said: That's alright, you're welcome. (pause)
Just one thing you could do for me?
She said: Certainly, what's that?
He said: If it's not too much trouble do you think you
could write me out a receipt?

L'Aventure

It isn't always Trevor Howard and Celia Johnson,
isn't always gourmet passion, five course and
overflowing with tears, turbulence and turmoil.

Sometimes it's convenience foods,
ready meals for the micro.
Something to tide you over
to fill a gap, fill a space
while
waiting for the chef to turn up.

Love and Passion

A wise man once said:
"Love is what's left
when the flames of passion die."

(Word of caution to avoid disappointment:
there may not be anything left)

More Romance

Elderly wife:	You've forgotten my valentine card
Elderly husband:	Oh yes so I have! Sorry about that. (Pause) Will you be my valentine?
Elderly wife:	Alright, yes I suppose so.
Elderly husband:	Right, well, that's settled that then.

Survival

They both said "I can't survive without you"
But she went one way and he went another
And they both survived.

Imaginative Seventy Something

- In a restaurant -

1st Man: Oh look there's a photo of Brigitte Bardot on the wall.
2nd Man: Yeah, she was another one who was always ringing up.
1st Man: Really?
2nd Man: Yeah, always on the phone. Kept saying Je t'aime and all that stuff.
1st Man: Really?
2nd Man Yeah I had to get my mum to tell her I was out a lot of the time.
1st Man: Really?
2nd Man: And of course there wasn't any laws about 'stalking' in those days.
1st Man: No. Tricky. So what did you do in the end?
2nd Man: Only thing I could do. Told her to 'push off'.

Routine

My life revolves around him.
He sets the pattern, provides the framework,
gives my life security.

Other influences more intimate and
direct, like the seasons, come and go.
Bring change and warmth, sometimes comfort,
other times gales, tempest, confusion.
But he, thank God, is a beacon.
Shining through the murk and haze of unpredictability.
Always there for me.

Usually his arrival is punctual but sometimes he's late
and it's then I realise his importance.
Feelings of insecurity and turmoil flood over me,
I can't do without him. Can't rest till he arrives.

Some tell me my reliance should be less enveloping,
His position in my life less elevated,
but he's my hero, my bringer of routine
and although I've never met him
I listen for his coming every Thursday.
His cheery expletives, often beginning with F,
drifting over the wall.

It's 'the rubbish man' that gives my life security,
everything collects around him.

Marriage and Democracy

- Finance -

Elderly Wife: I've got to phone the tax people about your tax.

Elderly Husband: Really! Well won't they want to speak to me.

Elderly Husband: Maybe but I'll tell them you're deaf and waiting for hearing aids.

Elderly man: Might be an idea to add that I've also got progressive senility. That should clinch it!

Elderly Wife: That's an idea.

- Later -

Elderly Husband: How did you get on?

Elderly Wife: They still insist on speaking to you.

Elderly Husband: Well if they start going on about finance I won't know what they're talking about.

Elderly Wife: Don't worry I'll be beside you. Just confirm who you are and then give the phone to me.

Elderly Husband: Do you want me to hang around?

Elderly Wife: No, no, that's OK. Nothing for you to worry about.

Elderly Husband: Fair enough! I'll do a bit of ironing!

Seasoned and Determined Traveller

Elderly Wife: Look, if I can have your trolley bed wheeled to the bottom of the stairs perhaps we can find some people to carry you onto the plane. What do you think?

Elderly Husband: Yes possibly! Failing that perhaps they could lift me into the hold so that I could travel with the baggage?

- brief pause -

Elderly Wife: That's an idea. I hadn't thought of that!!

Which is Which?

Elderly Husband: See those two pigeons? They could be male and female but how do you tell which is which?

Elderly Wife: I'm not sure.

Elderly Husband: Oh well never mind. I expect they know.

Elderly Wife: Almost certainly the female is the cleverer.

Elderly Husband: Maybe but more often than not the male is the prettier. The female is usually dowdy and frumpish!

Elderly Wife: Are you looking for a bunch of five?

Anticipation

She said:	Are you going to cut that loaf?
He said:	Yes, I am.
She said:	Then let me give you the breadboard.
He said:	Thank you. That's very thoughtful.
She said:	No not really, just saving a trip to A & E.

Wrong Again

He said:	If it wasn't for procreation and putting up the odd shelf you could probably do without us altogether?
She said:	Well, sorry but I'm afraid you're wrong again.
He said:	Really. How's that?
She said:	Most of us can put up our own shelves!

Just a Thought

They say when we die we spend
eternity with the person we most
loved.
So for some people
that could be a tricky decision.

PEOPLE

"You'll always be disappointed if you're polite and expect everyone else to be the same"

(*Nuffink in Particular Part One*, p68)

Secure

He sits on everything as though for eternity.
The museum he lives in; the possessions he rarely looks at;
most of the furniture he never sits on; the music he never
listens to; the toys he never plays with.
A life hoarded, embalmed, wrapped in dust, moribund.
Perhaps a hive with no interest in spring or summer.
No interest in production or distribution.

Like many
He belongs to a generation that followed the residue
or mists of penury; followed the 'one false move' to the
'work house' generation. 'No margin for error'.
Not for age, sickness or destitution.

"It could all be worth something one day.
People collect the old stuff don't they?
There's a market for old stuff. Old records, old furniture.
And some of it's in good condition.
Yes that's it. I'll put it up for sale".

But the days pass, the months pass, the years pass,
and the dust layers thicken and thicken on him
and his hive.

Dreams

Released onto winds of hope.
These are the blood of expectation.
Maybe the transport for life.
Maybe signposts for the journey.

Observe
Sometimes boundaries are close,
blowing on a gentle breeze.
They hug the comfort zone,
somewhere to live
work, marry, procreate,
to be happy in,
contained contentment.

Observe
Sometimes horizons far off,
dreams blown on strong winds,
focused and single minded winds
to the Albert Hall, to a Nobel Prize,
to winning 'The Ashes'

Then observe
Dreams blown off course
to meander, twist, turn,
to change direction.
Find other destinations.
The winds of fate.

Again observe
Dreams ravaged by storm,
plunging into Flanders mud,
into the tears of Tienanmen,
into a growth on the Pancreas.
Into extinction.

And finally observe
Dreams dissipated by time.
Diluted, watered down.
Filled with cynicism, pessimism.
Maybe displaced on children,
maybe onto self absorbed celebs.

"I could have been a contender Charlie"

Alone

They say we're born alone and die alone
Live in a patch of light
Move to where it moves
Until it gradually fades
Turns to amber
Grows over.

Loneliness

The pond is deep and dark
The water murky
Solitude is a mirror
Obscured

Genius

She said: I read the other day that Dickens behaved very badly to his wife.
He said: Yes I know.
She said: Forbade his children to see her.
He said: Yes apparently.
She said: But he was a genius wasn't he?
He said: Most people would say so.
She said: So I suppose that makes it alright then? His behaviour I mean!
He said: Well I ...!
She said: And Van Goff; sponged off his brother.
He said: Yes that's true.
She said: And Picasso said women were either 'goddesses or doormats'
He said: Yes, well...!
She said: Do you think it's possible to be a genius without being flawed?
He said: I'm not sure. Probably not!

Single Minded

He said: Phenomena's a violinist isn't she?
She said: Yes that's right and a very good one too I believe!
He said: So what's she like exactly?
She said: Well she's the sort of girl that can knock out Mendelssohn's violin concerto in E Minor Opus 64 at the drop of a hat but if she saw you with a hoover she'd wonder what it was for!!

A New Broom

Chairman: Thank you for electing me and may I say, to begin with, that I intend to be an all-inclusive chairman with the emphasis on involvement. Everyone can have their say and I welcome any opinions and advice. In other words the club will be run democratically with an opportunity for everyone to be engaged in the decision making process.

Member: I'm glad to hear you say that Mr. Chairman and I think I speak for everyone here when I say we welcome the opportunity to operate as a team. And especially when the chips are down you'll not find us wanting. We're behind you all the way.

- A few months later -

Member: If I may say so Mr. Chairman you've been looking a bit anxious lately. A bit stressed out. Any problems?

Chairman: Well yes! The truth is I've got a very difficult committee. There are some very opinionated people and lots of personality clashes. It really is very difficult to keep order at times. Any thoughts?

Member: No, not really. It's all to do with taking up the reins of office I'm afraid and at the end of the day, well, "You're in charge"!!

The Undergrowth

Thoughts, free and unstructured,
barge their way through the undergrowth.
An undergrowth already cluttered with debris,
decaying but only very slowly.

Well, no wait! It's not all slowly is it?
Some factual effluence can pass along quite quickly
with times, dates, appointments etc.
Sometimes consequential but mostly inconsequential
coming and going.

No, during one's life, it's 'images' that stick.
Get bogged down, lumber along, decay slowly
and always leave a trace.
Perhaps intimate moments, perhaps fearful moments,
attaching themselves, then drifting, then returning
but sometimes warming, of love or lust or both,
of childhood or achievement or compassion.
Still giving some comfort well into the undergrowth.

On the Bus

The young girl in front
lets down her hair and gathers it back up.
After a few minutes
she lets down her hair and gathers it back up.
After a few more minutes
she lets down her hair and gathers it back up
It's then one considers the possibility
that what she's doing
has nothing to do with hair.

Images

Images seeping in. On their own.
Triggered.
A word, mood, feeling.
Wanted, unwanted.
From the past but can be the present
To desire or fantasise desire

If wanted, try to hold on.
Unwanted, try to get rid of.

Sometimes so fleeting,
Childhood, a beach, laughing, crying,
A bed, passion, feeling, exploring.
Embracing
STAY,
Images of regret, cowardice, anger.
Unsettling.
GO...

Images of envy,
Jealousy of other's images.
To want others images. To covet them.
Should have been mine.
Should have been mine.

Images still to come?
Same format.

New Calendar

For an elderly person
A new calendar
Is like watching sand passing through a sieve.

Against the Tide

Determined to swim against the tide
Determined to resist change
Determined to maintain standards
He continued to use the semi-colon.

Or:
In order to challenge
 the laws of natural selection
(two fingers up to Darwin)
she deliberately
chose the runt of the litter.

Or:

Daughter:	Mum why don't you let me buy you an iPhone?
Mother:	Because I don't want one.
Daughter:	Well then at least a mobile phone. Just in case of an emergency.
Mother:	I don't need it! If I fall over in Canterbury there's a good chance somebody'll pick me up.

An Explanation

He said: I can't understand Jim? He's always so aggressive?
She said: Yes, he does seem to be.
He said: Whatever anyone says his first reaction is defensive. Trying to make smart remarks. Being cocky, being rude. Why do you think that is?
She said: Maybe it's all he's got going for him!

Repetition

To Covert
To Want
To Acquire
To Discard

People and Things

Celebration

And it came to pass that the Lord said to the faithful
"You have followed the scriptures so now you can go forth
into the highways and by-ways and enjoy yourselves.
Seek out happiness".
And there was great rejoicing throughout the land
and the multitude went forth into the highways and
by-ways and soon formed a great gathering.
And there was much merriment and feasting.
"Here is the promised harvest of happiness,
they said, abundant and plentiful,
We must take our fill".

But it came to pass
that soon there was no space for mules and carts
And soon there were great queues
And soon tempers were frayed
And babies were howling
And children were fighting
And grown-ups were arguing
And the noise was deafening
And it started to rain.

And the Lord became alarmed that his
people were becoming miserable
and falling into the ways of the ungodly.
But a group of the elders came and said
"Be not afeared Lord, your people are content
and much enjoyed the great gathering and hope
that in your wisdom there will be more such days.

The Lord was confused that they could
experience enjoyment in such strange ways
but it came to pass that he granted their wish
and said that every year they could have a small bank
of such days and henceforth they would be called
"Bank Holidays".
And the multitudes were much pleased
and there was great rejoicing and merriment
throughout the land.

The Comfort Zone

They wade in from either side
up to their waist but no further.
Further is not safe.
Sometimes they remember the challenge
to connect, to communicate, to touch.
They reach and stretch and strain but can't touch.
It's a ubiquitous but no longer obvious challenge
since there are the currents, the swell and the drift.
Obvious dangers...

Occasionally one moves forward but then
the other moves back. Afraid. Uncomfortable.
At one time they probably did meet without fear.
Younger, braver, less inhibited, less sanguine.
Prepared to take a chance.
But now they play safe. Up to the waist and no further.
Paddling is not enough, up to the chest is too far.

There are others up and down the stream.
Lots of others facing each other.
Most are up to their waist, not moving.
Only a few are connecting; physically,
mentally or both,
mostly the young but a few older ones.
For the rest, the majority, it's easy.
Within the 'comfort zone'.

The days pass with no great storms,
angry skies, tempests or thunder bolts
and they can sleep, undisturbed,
where they are.

If's and An's

Some people live in the past
Obsessively
Examine forensically
Lifting up memories and peering under them.

"What he said, what I said"
"What she did, what I did"

Or:
"What could have been"
"What should have been"
"What might have been"
But wasn't!

But why?

Because, Because...

The fate's decreed
The cards were stacked
The stars aligned
Against me.

Then onto another.
Poking about, shuffling round, sorting
and shifting, shifting and sifting
Through musty old tat.
Through musty old junk
Over and over
And round and round and round.
And round.

Sometimes justified
A major trauma
Memories so deep
Scars so deep
Difficult to move

But often
"If, 'If's and An's' were Pot's and Pan's
There'd be no work for Tinkers"!!*

*Nineteenth Century proverb

To Drivers

Be careful everyone
I'm the only imperfect driver
on the road.

Real Tough Guy

A real tough guy
takes on someone he
thinks he might lose to.

On Reflection

One remembers now
the
things one should have said but didn't
and the
things one did say but shouldn't have.

The Past

What's gone is gone.
Let the past sleep.
Wrap memories
warm memories
cradle them fondly
live with them
not in them.
For the rest
let them go

Old Dilemma

Sometimes
If only we could adjust time.
Rewind spiteful, penetrating words
spilling out, tumbling from the gut,
often irreversible.

Logic versus emotion. 'There's the rub'.
Whether to check and stop,
recruit reason, stay calm, bite the tongue...

Or to erupt,
to release lava, to spew from below, to
flow unplanned to destinations unconsidered,
to bury good soil, green roots, future life and
future possibilities

Of course
it could be just a trickle; repairable.
It could be necessary to realign,
to start afresh, to turn the worm.
To rebalance.

For some it's more the one.
For some it's more the other.

Always Certain

It's so comfortable to live within the walls of certainty,
to be always sure, to be always right.
To shelter safe and cosy from chill winds of doubt,
to be protected from the lingering frost of indecision.
So comfortable, so comforting,
the only path to follow.

Whatever the issue the answers are there
indexed, filed, cataloged, in easy reach,
available on request but often displayed
whether you want them or not.
An answer to fit every eventuality.

But then some say the buds never really open,
never really ripen or blossom or mature.
It's all there; all the ingredients are there;
an abundance of sun, rich soil, nutrients, moisture
all available but not admitted, stubbornly refused,
entry denied.

Instead the plant gathers sameness,
surrounded by sameness, seeking out sameness.
Seasons pass,
seasons come,
seasons go,
begin, end,
and nothing changes.

So comfortable, so comforting.

FRIENDS

"Friends are a gift from God to compensate for relatives."

Deleted

I just deleted the last photo of you.
The last record of you on a club walk.
You're in the distance but I know it's you.
The easily identified gait,
tall, relaxed, striding languid alongside the tree-line.
Your conversation, like the countryside, always expansive,
never inward, never introspective, always interested in
others.

And now you're deleted. Twice in fact.
Once from the earth and now from my computer.

But it's pragmatism that rules the decision.
You see I'm trying to declutter, spring clean the desk top.
Alright so now there's a shadow of guilt
creeping up, drifting round.
But you must understand
we can't be recorded forever.

Priorities

1st Supporter	I'm afraid I'll have to miss the game next month. My novel's been short listed for the 'Booker Prize' so I've got to go to the Savoy Hotel.
2nd Supporter	You realise we're playing at home to 'Maidstone'. A local derby!
1st Supporter	Yes I know. Sorry.
2nd Supporter	And it's a crunch game. A lot riding on it. A chance to go up the league?
1st Supporter	Yes I know.
2nd Supporter	Talk about a fair weather supporter. No good the lads relying on you.
1st Supporter	Sorry
2nd Supporter	Have you told Archie and Reg. I don't know what they're gonna say?

(pause)

1st Supporter	Alright I'll phone the 'Booker' people and tell them I can't make it!
2nd Supporter	So you're coming then?
1st Supporter	Yes alright.
2nd Supporter	I should think so too!

Priorities 2

1st Man: Your back then?
2nd Man: Yeah, got back last night.
1st Man: Have a good holiday?
2nd Man: It was OK until the day before yesterday when I fell down some steps and smacked my face on the pavement.
1st Man: Oh dear!
2st Man: Yeah, blood everywhere, ambulance, hospital, stitches; the lot.
1st Man: Oh dear!
2nd Man: Yeah! Still painful and I look a mess with a black eye, bruises and bandages.
1st Man: Oh dear! (pause) Does this mean you're not coming over the football?

A Point of View

Young Barmaid:	Have you been walking?
Rambler:	Yes I have.
Young Barmaid:	What round here. Up in the hills?
Rambler:	Yes, that's right.
Young Barmaid:	How far have you walked?
Rambler:	Oh about six miles.
Young Barmaid:	SIX MILES!! That's a long way?
Rambler:	Well about two and a half hours.
Young Barmaid:	TWO AND A HALF HOURS!!
Rambler:	Roughly
	(Pause)
Young Barmaid:	I don't do walking.
Rambler:	No?
Young Barmaid:	No I don't like it. It's boring and it wears me out.
Rambler:	That's a pity but if you ever change your mind you can always come walking with our group?
Young Barmaid:	No thanks, I've seen your group.
Rambler:	What do you mean?
Young Barmaid:	Look no offence but I wouldn't be seen dead walking with a load of old people!

Gadgets

Two elderly lady ramblers.

1st Lady: He's a funny bloke that Brian. Always walks along holding that thing.
2nd Lady: You mean his gadget.
1st Lady: That's it. Always holding it.
2nd Lady: Yes I've noticed.
1st Lady: And sometimes he stops and looks at it.
2nd Lady: Yes he does.
1st Lady: Stares at it.
2nd Lady: I know.
1st Lady: Sometimes for ages.
2nd Lady: I know.
1st Lady: I think he's obsessed with it.
2nd Lady: So do I.

Colds! What to do?

- on the telephone -

1st man: Are you meeting us down the pub?
2nd man: No I've got a cold so I think I'll give it a miss.
1st man: That's a bit 'wimpish' isn't it?
2nd man: Do you think so?
1st man: A lame excuse I'd say.
2nd man: Right! Well I'll come then.

- Later -

2nd man: Hello, are you alright? I haven't seen you for a few days.
1st man: No I'm not alright. I'm nearly dying.
2nd man: What's the problem then?
1st man: I've got your flipping cold that's what! I can't go out or do anything.
2nd man: Sorry to hear that.
1st Man: People should keep their colds to themselves. Not go around giving them to other people.

Worth Knowing

1st Man: Did I tell you I've got a new next door neighbour.

2nd Man: No, really? What's he like, or should I say she?

1st Man: He actually. Oh average height, bit on the stout side, about forty.

2nd Man: No I mean what's he like?

1st Man: He's friendly, seems to enjoy his garden, feeds the birds. Seems very pleasant.

2nd Man: No I mean what's his interests? What does he do? Who does he know? Has he written anything? Painted anything? Into politics? Know any politicians?

1st Man: I'm not sure! Why do you want to know?

2nd Man: Well, is he the sort of person one could invite to dinner? Introduce to friends? What car does he drive?

1st Man: Um, a Ford Fiesta I think.

2nd Man: Forget it.

Les

You so wanted to stay with us
So wanted to live and plan
and find new paths, new challenges.
To fill and to pack all the crevices
of every minute of every hour of every day.

And you did not "go gentle into that good night"
but fought bravely and fiercely and
"raged, raged against the dying of the light."*
And even when all hope seemed lost and
the storm clouds gathered and gathered
you so wanted to stay.

But know
that when we hear the wind passing through
the trees and when we watch the sun set on a
neighbouring hillside and when we pass a stream
slowly meandering softly and gently on it's way
you have stayed with us
in our minds and in our hearts.

Les died of covid. September 2021

* 'Do Not Go Gentle Into That Good Night' - Dylan Thomas

Last Week

We lived in bedsits, in a large Victorian house, in
Barnes, not far from the river Thames

And last week we walked along the river and
stopped to watch the university boat race.
Cambridge won.

And last week Pat slogged his working way to
London and Peter and I trudged our way to a, not
very inspiring, teacher training course.

And last week, in the evening, we went to the Bulls
Head and watched Phil Seaman on the drums and
Blossom Dearie sing the blues.

And last week we laughed when the roof leaked
and the landlord generously gave us a bucket and
everyone searched for a shilling for the meter.

And last week, in the evening, Pat played his guitar,
while Peter painted and I read a book about cricket.

'And last week' Pat died on September 6th and Peter
died on September 7th - fifty three years later.

Cause and Effect

He said: Have you seen Jane and Mary lately?
She said: No I haven't and it's a bit awkward because
they've fallen out.
He said: Really, I thought they were bosom pals.
She said: That's right they were.
He said: So what happened then? It must be serious.
Men, money, work?
She said: No nothing like that.
He said: So what then?
She said: They went on holiday together.

TRAVEL

"A journey of a thousand miles begins with a single step"

- unless you trip over! -

Ancient Chinese proverb
by Philosopher Lao Tzu

Jacaranda

Returning from Nice in a year now forgotten
I planted a tray of hope.
Black seeds, from a bulging black pod,
flat and spilling into and under
a rich, fertile, blanket of incubation.
And waited, with tempered optimism,
for a coming. For an awakening.

And later,
with the warmth of spring, arrived
just one recruit from an army of hopefuls
reaching up from the dark, pushing for the light,
straining for life.

And then later,
not in infancy, more in adolescence.
Placed in a pot, covered with compost and June sun
for the roots to travel. To explore. To spread…
I hoped.

And then, later still, in expectation,
to become tall and handsome and green and cocky
and show off its bunches of blue beauty,
to the world.
To be my pride and joy.

Today, all the above was long ago,
it resides in a large pot,
in the summer outdoors
in the winter indoors.
Still alive and green but suspended in adolescence,
no bunches of blue.
And me too soft to vote for its disposal.

The Feria de Seville

It's held every April and lasts for a week,
a gilded occasion honed over decades
and by anyone's judgment a 'spectacle'.
'Image' matched by 'reality'.

It's an 'Andalusian Institution' with people
coming from far and near.
A large area set aside, "Los Remedios" with
dozens of tents, parties every night, eating,
singing, flamenco dancing and
mucho vino.

The festival taxi's are numerous.
Horse drawn carriages with men in sombreros,
usually Grey; short jackets and the horses
with tassels and garlands on mane and
platted tails.
Todo es muy grapo.

Most striking are the ladies of all ages
and girls in their traditional dress.
So many colours with layers of frills at the bottom
and on the arms and a flower, artificial,
on top of the head.

Some, with hair severely platted or collected
into a bun could sit comfortably into a print
of times long gone. Sitting with
'Hemingway' in the 1930's.

With others, perhaps more modern, one might
catch a glimpse of trainers or 'I' phones or
'a fag' or imagine them saying:
"Lets get on with it. It's Feria time again.
Time to get the gear out and get glamnmed up.
Do a bit of posing. Check out the opposition".

The week soon passes.
Then the clear-ups under way.
The costumes put away.
The vendors, horses, visitors all gone home.
All crystallized.
All suspended,
until metamorphosed once again next year.

The Language Student

1st Man: How are you getting on with the Spanish?
2nd Man: Oh, ok I suppose.
1st Man: That doesn't sound very positive?
2nd Man: Well, some of it's ok.
1st Man: But you know a lot of words
2nd Man: Oh yes I do.
1st Man: And all the verbs and tenses?
2nd Man: Oh yes, I know all that.
1st Man: So what's the problem then?
2nd Man: Well I'm ok so long as no-one starts talking to
me!

Enlightenment

In Salamanca herds of school pupils
are driven daily to selected pastures,
considered to be rich, nutritious and beneficial,
for them to feed on and devour,
hopefully,
copious amounts of enlightenment.

One such herd,
Espanoles, mixed gender, around fifteen years of age,
are tethered in the square facing the old 14th century
university building with it's facade, 'muy famosa'.
A 'profesora' of the enlightenment is feeding
the herd with information.
Encouraging the digestion of 'muchas historias'.

But unfortunately
one notices, the herd, as a whole,
seems to be somewhat disengaged.
Some are chatting and giggling.
Some, with iPhones are clearly
more interested in other forms of nourishment.
While some, one suspects,
with blank expressions, are currently visiting
pastures on a completely different planet,
in a completely different solar system.

The one exception, standing out,
is a 'chico' pointing out to 'su amigo'
some significant aspect of the facade.
And both, most gratifyingly,
displaying signs of genuine interest.

Suddenly, without any prior warning
the herd comes together,
goes into a huddle and after a moment
leaps into the air as one,
arms outstretched to the heavens,
and shout
'OLE'
Then back into the huddle only
to repeat the exercise moments later.
'OLE'

With an exchange of glances
the 'profesora' offers a grin that overlays embarrassment
followed by a 'what can one do' shrug.
One responds sympathetically,
appreciating and remembering the forces of opposition
laying in wait for even the most committed profesora.

Later, on reflection,
one questions the wisdom of moving the herd in this fashion
and its non-productive search for enlightenment!
Could it be an exercise more correctly labeled
"A waste of time"?

But then one ponders,
is this opinion over critical, over analytic?
After all there was the one 'chico'
and 'su amigo' who seemed genuinely interested
and who knows if the others have somewhere stored
memories of these pastures for later visitation.

Also, and perhaps 'muy importante',
they all seemed to be enjoying themselves.

Big Problem

Robinson Crusoe
on his desert island in the eighteenth century,
before Man Friday showed up
with an abscess under his tooth!!

Cracking an Egg

Cracking an egg into the frying pan
suddenly I'm back in the New York diner,
which in commonplace mirrors the whole.
A daily breakfast with
a frantic, neurotic, hysterical, never ceasing hair dryer.
Buzz, Buzz, Buzz.
Over easy, sunny side up, benedict, maple syrup, waffles
then into the street
jams, car horns, traffic cops, shouts, resignation, aggression.
Rush, Rush, Rush.
The mayor brings in anti 'road rage' laws!
Says on TV "driving on the roads is a privilege
not a place to act out childish fantasies"!
The next day,
was anyone else watching TV?

Valencia

As palm leaves sway in a gentle breeze a lado la playa
and the floating housing estates, sometimes
referred to as 'cruise liners' tie up in Valencia harbour
so it seems most young Spaniards speak and wish
to practice speaking Ingles.
'Dos billetos por el proximo partido' I confidently ask
the young hombre selling football tickets.
He responds in Spanish but after a brief conversation
and as I stumble over a few words he suddenly says
"Actually I do speak English" and worst still
"I would have mentioned it earlier but I was just
enjoying listening to your Spanish."
Argh

And so into the cafe and before a 'Quisera' is offered up
the senorita's "What can I get you" only needs a "dear"
to transport the whole scene to a cafe in Herne Bay.
Also "I'll just get you the menu in English" hammers
yet another nail into an already fragile coffin.
Argh

At the end of the meal and after taking the order for
'desert' she inquires "can I bring you coffee"?
Now an opportunity to recover some ground presents
itself as I mumble "at the moment I'm not sure."
She hesitates, clearly uncertain. There's a chance; I pounce:
"En este momento, no seguro".
She's wrong footed. Could it be a triumph?
Yes but only for a second as she quickly re-groups.
"No problem. I'll come back when your ready"
Argh

Morale at a low ebb I sit on a park bench
to lick my wounds in peace and quiet.
No such luck as three young 'pain in the bums' appear with
'ello', 'ow are you', ''Tottingham Hosper', 'Manhester United'
and other infantile remarks.
How can they know with such certainty I'm English?
With no reaction they soon get bored and wander off
but not before 'ave a nice day' and 'hodbye'.
Argh

In conclusion be warned,
the 'estudiante de Espanyol' trying to play a straight bat
is really up against it.

Walking in County Mayo

Following the old coach road along a bleak,
mountainous, rock strewn avenue of beauty,
sheep representing life and painted unconcerned,
almost stationary, into the landscape, the guide book
told me it was once home to many poor families.
Also that with no great effort I can still see the ruin of
one such dwelling and nearby its wave like contours
of poor sod given over to the growing of potatoes.

It soon appeared and as I stood and stared, thoughts
meandered as to how anyone could survive in such
a harsh and barren place, even in good times, and
how God or fate or both had connived with nature,
to deal out such an unforgiving hand.

But then as I looked, suddenly the dwelling becomes
complete. It's no longer a ruin but now a cottage,
perhaps hovel a better description, and I can see
the potato ridges clearly defined, fresh dug.

And from the door emerges eight to ten children,
or walking bundles of rags, a better description,
hands outstretched,
bloated bellies, hollows where eyes should be
and such despair and desperation as they
move towards me.
Best not to look but of course compulsively one does.

And now in the doorway stand the parents, at least
I assume that's who they are, equally emaciated
and pointing to brown mushy inedible heaps.

It's a pitiful sight this cul de sac of options,
this absence of alternatives, absence of escape.
But then suddenly in the distance a car horn sounds,
a voice shouts, the i-phone bleeps and
the images start to fade or drift back into history,
a better description.

An Incident

The steps leading down from the church seemed
friendly enough but contained, unbeknownst to me,
a secret initiative test. To reach the bottom unscathed.
Sadly the records will show a miserable failure
and inability to reach the required standard on my part
as the unforgiving pavement rose up to embrace,
with little or no resistance, my soft and accommodating
forehead. A deep gash above the eyebrow!

Alarm and mayhem.
Then voices; concerned voices.
Then more voices as a mini audience assembled
and clearly I was in the middle of a 'mise en scene'
playing the principal, reluctant and bewildered, character.

Minor parts, soon cast, included an angelic female
who appeared with a first aid kit, used to great effect;
a bearded policeman peering down who reminded
me of Popeye's long time adversary 'Bluto' and an
ambulance driver who at first seemed as sympathetic
as the pavement but later showed that to be a temporary
aberration and was most kind and helpful.

Wheeled in on a trolley, with no fanfare, exposure to
A&E revealed a sea of humanity who, one suspected,
were not recently engaged as extras but were real people.
Mostly elderly with one or two younger, possible drug addicts,
one or two workman, encased in bandages and splints and
looking remarkably like those characters seen in the old 'tabloid'
cartoons and nearly everyone, like me, the victims of similar
unprovoked initiative tests.

With few exceptions, one or two in wheelchairs, the majority were on trolley beds and interestingly placed in rows facing the two, sliding door, treatment rooms. One couldn't help but speculate, in a moment of acute boredom, that any moment a gun would be fired to initiate an Olympic style dash to medical salvation and thus reveal the gold medal winner and Usain Bolt of A&E 'trolley bed sprinting'. Four hours later and the above mentioned fantasy, long since abandoned, I finally entered the treatment room.

The young doctor seemed very pleasant and remarkably cheerful for someone who'd spent several hours under siege but his attendant nurse proved a quite different proposition. In appearance a tough beefy creature, who looked as if a career in professional boxing represented a missed opportunity, she proceeded to rip off my temporary dressing, now firmly cemented in place with congealed blood, with dismissive ferocity.

The same delicacy of touch was applied to cleaning up the wound and I was severely reprimanded for flinching every time she biffed my forehead with a straight jab.

Thankfully the insertion of stitches went off without too many alarms although it was later decided that two more connectors were needed by which time the local anaesthetic had worn off. Not a pleasant experience….

After six memorable hours I left the hospital covered in temporary bandages, held in place by an elastic stocking which, fastened under the chin, looked not unlike 'the invisible man' in those moments when he was not invisible.

We returned to the hotel and flew home the next day with the acquired sagacity that A&E in Vienna is, by anecdotal accounts, not very different to what it is here!

The Goodwin's

Standing on the Goodwin sands
there are lives, under your feet,
lungs that breathed, hearts that beat
moments of terror, hours of anguish
all folded into the sand and now
embalmed, entombed, incarcerated
under your feet.
Today, except for a few seals,
a few kittiwakes, a few gulls
it’s all so peaceful, so uneventful
it could be any strip of sand
anywhere.

SOCIAL ISSUES

"Man is not an island unto himself"

John Donne

Musing on the Issue

He said: After Brexit do you think there'll be no more
bluebirds over the White Cliffs of Dover?
She said: There never were any bluebirds. They don't exist
here. It's an American bird!
He said: Well alright then, what about 'love and laughter
and peace ever after'. Do you think they'll go?
She said: What are you talking about? I don't know.
Why are you asking me all this?
He said: I just wondered if they'd go to Frankfurt or Paris
along with everything else?
She said: Silly old duffer.

Old Industries

They said:
Don't worry they'll be back. What comes around
goes around.
When the smoke rises and the wars start, they'll
be back.
But...
There have been many wars and ships and steel
and coal and smoke rising
And they haven't come back
And...
Now they're parked in far away places where
the great God of the Market rules,
(with a firm hand)
And says...
Now they must be in charge
And says...
Now it's their turn to grow and expand and kill
everything, everywhere.

Into the Future

- Boy looking at historic picture book -

Boy: Dad where did all the elephants go?

Dad: Oh they were bumped off a long time ago for the ivory trade. Made things from those tusks. Might be one or two left somewhere. I'm not sure.

Boy: And what about these. Are they rhino's and tiger's?

Dad: That's right. They were bumped off as well to make medicines in China and places. None of those left.

Boy: And these creatures?

Dad: They're polar bears. They gradually disappeared when the ice caps melted. A lot of islands and parts of countries went as well. Shame.

Boy: Yeah. Couldn't they stop it?

Dad: Well they probably could have but they were too late. People were more interested in making money and running cars and in the end it had gone too far. For a while there were even people running countries who said it wasn't happening!

Boy: What were these places?

Dad: Oh they were called shops. People used to buy things from them.

Boy: What things?

Dad: Stuff to eat. Clothes to wear. Whatever you wanted. They gradually disappeared when people ordered 'on line'. It was cheaper so they stopped going to shops.

Boy: And all these trees. Lots of them together.

Dad: Yeah, they were called forests and the bigger ones were called jungles. It took a long time to get rid of them but they got there in the end.

Boy: They look nice! Why did they do that?

Dad: To build houses and factories. Make money. Make people rich. A lot of animals disappeared as well because they lived in the forest. Still a few bits left.

Boy: More shops?

Dad: No they were called 'Post Offices'. People use to send letters and parcels; buy stamps. All different things. They were owned by the country. Run by the government.

Boy: Disappeared as well?

Dad: Yeah, closed down. Not making enough money so sold to people to run privately and they gradually went altogether.

Boy: And this one?

Dad: Oh they were called monkeys. They lived mostly in Africa and people killed them to eat when they were hungry. I think there are still a few of those left.

Boy: This is a type of bird?

Dad: They were called swallows. They disappeared with a lot of other birds when their habitats went and the insects died off. A lot of other birds disappeared as well.

Boy: This is a mountain.

Dad: That's right. It's called Mount Everest. It's the highest mountain in the world. It use to be covered in snow but that all melted.

Nasty Army

Occasionally even the most strident optimist
who peers into the microscope of imagination
can see cells; nasty little cells. Somnambulists
Beginning to stir; beginning to wake. Somnambulists
No longer moribund, no longer dormant.

And slowly as one watches, with anxiety,
they're starting to move, searching for life.
And gradually as one watches, with alarm,
they've started recruiting, building an army.
"They're on the move"!!

And it's an evil army with limited objectives.
Moving with purpose to subjugate, dominate, destroy.
Ultimately the entire entity, including themselves,
fanatics ready to die for the cause.

So now we look for the defenders, the good cells,
to see them rally, challenge evil, resist the invaders.
But they're docile, watching, doing nothing,
just pottering about while the menace grows.
"Wake up"!! "Wake up"!!

Remind them of Burke's warning: revised,
"The only thing necessary for the triumph of evil
is for good cells to do nothing"
But still they ignore. Still make no effort.
It seems a lost cause

So now one must look for help from outside,
powerful enough to kill the parasites
or at least reduce their number.
Powerful enough to restore order
or at least reach equilibrium.

There is hope
but
it's a long road
and
many are lost along the way.

Don't Blame History

History can explain the journey
show the path
describe the arrival
but then
the choices are ours.

Equilibrium

Everything seems out of balance
No symmetry
No harmony
No Palladian structure

Between altruism and avarice
Creation and distribution
Have and have nots.
Young and old
Quick witted and slow witted
Savvy and non savvy.

"It's always been thus" I hear you shout!
Perhaps but
Have fissures become chasms?
Cracks become canyons?
The pit become a gorge?

Methinks
"There's something cock-eyed somewhere".

An obvious path

Teacher: Trying to teach you English is virtually impossible. You just never pay attention!

Pupil: Yeah I know but all that stuffs no use to me; I'm gonna join the merchant navy.

Management

(Telephone rings)

Secretary: Hello, Buckley College of Further Education. Business and Secretarial Department. Mrs Drinkwater speaking. Can I help you?

Enquirer: Oh hello, yes, I'd like to enquire about courses in management? Do you have any?

Secretary: Oh yes, certainly, we run several courses; both daytime and evening. Do you have anything particularly in mind?

Enquirer: Yes, I'm looking for a course with emphasis on management and future planning.

Secretary: Oh dear! No, I'm afraid that's not possible!

Enquirer: Really! Why not?

Secretary: Because all our courses focus on 'crisis management'. Nothing to do with the future.

Enquirer: Oh dear.

Secretary: Yes and what's more I think you'll have great difficulty finding anyone who offers that sort of thing. No demand I'm afraid.

Poem to a Friend

It's true I'm somewhat becalmed under a
mist of melancholia at the moment.
And it's true that a segment of this condition
can be traced to the detritus of ageing.
Paddling around in stagnant memories,
raking over festering times past.

But really the largest melancholic chunk comes
from constant exposure to the daily news of stabbings,
bombings, destruction of nature, torture etc. etc. etc.
and the realisation that parcels of optimism are both
thin on the ground and miniscule by comparison.
So...
the only solace or amelioration of this condition
is to reach for my pen
or
switch off the tele!!

The Proof

MP:	I want to thank you for inviting me here today to answer any questions and concerns you might have. So lets start by asking if…Ah, yes sir?
Elderly Man:	I feel uncomfortable every time I go out of my front gate.
MP:	And why is that?
Elderly Man:	Well for one thing it's not safe. I've seen a woman get her bag snatched and a boy smash a car window. And the other week a bloke got stabbed outside the pub down the road.

MP: Really! Anything else?

Elderly Man: Yes, last week I went for a hospital appointment and when I got there all I could see was people. Some had been there for ages and they weren't happy. And then it started to turn nasty so I came away.

MP: Oh dear!

Elderly Man: It was the young doctor and the nurses I felt sorry for. Trying to cope.

MP: I see.

Elderly Man: And another thing! What about all these young people sleeping rough with nowhere to live and all the people using the food banks? It's looking like the 1930's

MP: Thank you sir for sharing your concerns but let me try to put your mind at rest.

Elderly Man: Go on then.

MP: Well, first of all Government statistics clearly show that overall, year on year, crime is coming down.

Elderly Man: Really!

MP: Yes and secondly, they also show hospital waiting times are coming down as well. The service is improving.

Elderly Man: Well, I never!

MP: And finally unemployment is at a record low so there's plenty of opportunity for young people and new house building schemes usually include affordable housing. So does that help to allay your fears?

Elderly Man: I don't know. It's difficult to say. Do you think it would help if I changed my gate?

The Worried Well

The worried well are worried still
because they think they might be ill.
They sit around and muse all day on
aches and pains that come their way.
Of ailments that they have no doubt
will be the ones to see them out.

So to the doctors they all go,
regale them with their tales of woe.
To have them listen with concern
so hopefully they can discern
some treatment that can be prescribed,
designed to keep them all alive.

I'm losing weight they groan and say.
I'm losing height is that alright?
And when I pee there is poor flow
A PSA will surely show
a bigger problem lurking there
and a need for constant care.

The doctors think it right to tell
their worried patients that they're well.
They say with calmness and sobriety
there is no cause for their anxiety.
But all entreaties they do fail
and pleading is of no avail

"Don't try to fob us off," they say.
"We know the game you're trying to play.
Of one thing we are very sure,
we could be dying and what's more
you must treat us; that's the law."

So now the creams and tablets flow
into a bottomless pit they go.
That's called the NHS we know.
The x'rays and the scans abound.
Of course no problem can be found.

Appeased the worried well retreat.
But
no discomfort in defeat.
Tomorrow brings another day
and lots more worries to come their way.

A Christmas Carol

It's raining outside and inside
one ponders on the landscape of things to come,
or maybe the spectre of things to come.
A la 'A Christmas Carol'.

We're looking for trees bearing 'well-being'?
It's not easy!
Trees laden with optimism, bulging with 'hope';
fat branches holding security!!
Really, feel good trees for everyone,
harvested over months and decades,
maybe even centuries.

Can you make out acquisitive trees?
They're easy to spot.
Well positioned, in rich soil, no need for fertiliser,
with branches so full of finance and consumption.
Full of things and things and more things.
In the right climate they're solid, dependable,
high yield bearing and planted early,
they're strong from the beginning.

And what of trees elsewhere? e.g. in Africa.
Again they're easy to spot.
Poor soil, little water, struggling.
Laden with poverty, bulging with suffering for
people and animals. For all living things
as far as the eye can see.
They're dying bit by bit.

Let's call on the ghost of things to come.
To call on Scrooge to plant more trees.
To save the people and elephants, rhino's
and polar bears and so on and so on and so on.

Is there a chance?
One thinks only a slim one because
not many people believe in or listen to ghosts!

Balance Sheet

Ideally,
When crossing the Rubicon
there should be a balance sheet for evil
and ideally evil should know there's a balance sheet;
know there's an out-tray of retribution waiting patiently
just off stage, in the wings,
to conclude the final business; the final transaction.
Dot your nasty i's and cross your nasty t's.

Eliminate thoughts of immortality. You will die.
Dismiss notions of forgiveness. The fatted cow with
all the trimmings. The prodigal murderer returned.
Forget 'I was only following orders Gov'
or 'I did it for God'. The oldest of fallbacks.

Know that your customers are waiting! In line!
Waiting to offer the same fear, the same pain,
the same anguish you dished out
Only now multiplied
and stretched
and stretched
and stretched on forever.

Ideally.

Darkness in Afghanistan August 2021

Let the darkness fall
with its baggage of hatred and subjugation.
Let it cover the children, their teachers,
their classroom and the waiting women.
Women waiting. Women trembling.
Let the sun retreat behind the mountains
so nothing can live, nothing worthwhile in
a landscape of bigotry and cruelty.
Let the brief pool of enlightenment now shrink,
and fester, decay and grow stagnant in the
houses, and in the streets, and the towns
and the cities and the memories and the minds.
Let there be no compassion.
Let the warmth of engagement grow cold.
Let the people in far off lands watch, observe
and feel helpless.

The Origins August 2021

I remember
The decisions were made by death hiding in the hills
above Afghanistan.
I remember
The decisions were made by death swinging from the
crossbar in the football stadium.
I remember
Death absorbing stones with no help or comfort from
onlookers and bystanders.
All in the distant past, all in distant lands
but
I remember how it started.

Edvard Munch The Scream June 2021

It could be a thousand faces
Screaming with pain, with grief, with despair
A thousand universal faces. Anywhere, anytime.
the past, present, known, unknown,
Screaming

But having watched the news,
This is the face of a Palestinian woman
And she's screaming for her dead child.
And it's an inconsolable face
etched with pain, lined with grief,
overflowing with despair and desperation.
Screaming

And now it's a face embarked on a journey
an irreversible journey of repetition and replay.
For this woman there's no relief in words,
no solace in time, no salvation in the hereafter.
She will live the brutal bare reality of a moment,
frozen in time, over and over again.
This woman's screaming forever.

And what of the bystanders.
Removed, detached. Hands in pockets.
Are these the universal bystanders?
Detached with discomfort bystanders?
Watching, observing, reporting.
Shielding for safety
and not screaming.

The Benefactor

He said: It's time we got back to some basic principles in this country.
She said: Such as?
He said: Fairness, redistribution of wealth, standing up for the underdog. Giving people a chance.
She said: I couldn't agree more but how do you square that with 'buy to let'?
He said: How do you mean?
She said: Well you own three properties you rent out!!
He said: That's right. I provide people with a place to live. A roof over their heads.
She said: And you have a second home that's empty most of the time.
He said: That's right but I employ someone to maintain it for me not to mention the opportunity for the building industry to add an extension. So I'm creating employment.
She said: I see, so you're a benefactor really?
He said: Yes that's right. Of course I am …

As an Elderly Person

As an elderly person
Sometimes I just want to coast in
Sometimes search only for tranquil waters
Sometimes ignore and hide from everything
But can't.

NATURE

*"You don't have to like other living creatures,
just try not to be cruel to them."*

The Ringwould Yew

Omnipotent yew
Now you're one thousand, three hundred years old
surely you can't still remember being planted.
Can't remember being a sapling or growing or swelling,
swallowing up centuries, absorbing decades,
spreading and spreading, season after season.

Surely you can't remember the thousands of feet that
have trodden past you in different times, in different garbs.
Some plodding, some rushing, some working, some praying.
Surely in your life they're like puffs of wind blowing past;
blowing on a gentle breeze. So brief you'd hardly notice.

And surely you've seen so much happiness
and so much sorrow. Repeated and repeated.
And what of the children? Laughing and crying and
fighting and chasing each other under your canopy?
Can you remember any of them?

And then later, so many of those who passed by
now resting under you and you feeding from them.
Your roots spreading and pushing into their nourishment.
Into the flesh and bones of those you once saw.

You're just a shell now. You look so old
There's a hollow where your trunk once stood.
You're a gnarled, crusted, fragmented shell.
But alive?
Oh still so very much alive.
Omnipotent yew.

Tiny John

An adopted, small, black cat with
a hole in the heart.
Both physically and metaphorically.

By nature T J was a vagabond;
roaming, by choice, the local highways and byways,
aloof and disdainful of interaction, except when
necessary to defend himself and to all recorded
observation an independent spirit if ever there was one.

Many labelled him anti-social and some insisted part feral,
citing as evidence the scratch and bite marks inflicted on
those with tactile intentions. But he'd reply:
"You leave me alone and I'll leave you alone"
The vet always wore gloves.

Only after a few days absence, when his tummy clock
ticked over to food, would he let himself in, via the
cat flap and adopting a really stroppy, grumpy demeanour
stand quite motionless and demand,
or more accurately howl, for sustenance.

One recalls, returning home late one evening,
TJ sitting in the gloom, in the hallway,
staring at us intently as if to say:
"What time do you call this?
What's going on? My bowl's empty and
I've been sitting here waiting and starving
for hours while you two pushed off.
It's not good enough."

Eventually, during the hot August of 2004,
his heart succumbed and he would roam no more.
He lay, stretched out under a shrub, stiff as a board
with an angelic as opposed to his usual bolshy expression
and as I was burying him, wrapped in muslin,
a friend arrived and expressed her sympathy.
I replied: " He was a stroppy, miserable, anti-social little sod
and I'll miss him like hell"!!

Fred

Our cat died last week.
And I know
He was 'only a cat'.
And I know
It was insignificant
'Globally'
And I know
There's suffering everywhere
'Everyday'
But it was Fred
Who sat on our laps
Loved his kisses and cuddles,
Loved his chin rubbed,
Being in his garden,
Being combed.
And it was Fred
Who was woven into our lives
For twelve years.

An Autumn Day

A beautiful warm autumn day. Sitting in the arbour
filling our faces with pineapple and coconut cake,
we observe in close proximity the prettiest of tiny mice;
perfectly formed with eyes and ears moulded in symmetry,
completely ignoring and indeed oblivious to our presence.
It could have been a 'he' but was most likely, as
possessing such complete and heavenly attributes, a 'she'.

And what a busy 'she' she was.
Weaving in and out of the amber and red leaves,
disappearing and reappearing, searching and foraging.
Hardly stopping and finally discovering bird seed
deposited on the path by our resident, voracious
gang of sparrows who, without consulting any reference
books on etiquette or more specifically table manners,
eject from the bird feeder an amount of seed
roughly equivalent to half that consumed.
Most interestingly mouse and sparrow seem to
have established an entente cordial as they
munch away quite happily side by side.

One couldn't help but conjecture, rather morbidly,
that her fate might be linked with a cat, fox, or bird of pray
but with luck old age still has to be a possibility.

A moment later a small bird appears, again in close
proximity and again without any regard to our presence.
It hops around the shrub from branch to branch
looking this way and that; quite deliberately.

"That's a young sparrow" I confidently assert.
"No it's a young robin" counters my wife!
"But it hasn't got a red breast"
"Young robins don't have red breast's"
"And how do you know Mrs Expert ?" I cross- examine.
"You're forgetting I joined the U3A Natural History Group"
"We often see them"
Knowledge based on empirical evidence is hard to refute.
So...
'Game set and match'.

Journey's End

Stopping over on this beautiful Mediterranean island
I woke this morning feeling refreshed, restored
and ready for the long flight home.
There to build my nest, find my mate,
have my babies, feed them, watch them grow,
ensure the species, ensure the future.

You woke this morning and decided,
with your rifle and nothing better to do,
to ensure none of this would happen.

Mr Sparrow

In the garden
In the arbour
A beautiful hot July day
A washing up bowl
Half full of water

A sparrow floating on the surface
Floating peacefully,
Floating gently,
Hardly moving.

I see a tragedy
I see misjudgement
Attempted refreshment
Waterlogged wings

I see panic
A frantic struggle
A desperate struggle
A threshing fight for life

I see it gradually fading
less frantic
less desperate
Slowly ebbing
Slowly, slowly, slowly ebbing
into exhaustion.
Into floating
peacefully on the surface.

I know the scenario Mr Sparrow
I know the sequence Mr Sparrow,
I've been there Mr Sparrow
The only difference is
I was rescued and you weren't.

Time for a Change

Mr Squirrel:	Hello, you're looking a bit fed up?
Mr Rat:	Yes well I am. No one seems to like me and I don't know why? I try to keep myself to myself. Keep away from the humans. Not upset anyone.
Mr Squirrel:	Yes I've noticed.
Mr Rat:	You're lucky. You don't seem to have too many problems?
Mr Squirrel:	No I don't really and people see much more of me than they do of you!
Mr Rat:	Any suggestions?
Mr Squirrel:	Well yes. Have you thought of growing a bushy tail!

The Evergreen

From the bedroom window
A grey sky.
A grey day.
A grey mood.
Everything in harmony.

Or it should be,
but it's not!

Where there should be a drab vista
through skeletal trees
drizzling over deserted tennis courts
there's a large evergreen full of leaves.
It's obscuring my mood.
How dare this tree ruin my mood!
Chop it down at once.

I'm changing my mind about the evergreen,
it seems to be a gathering place for birds,
a piazza without so much posing.

Sparrows move around in gangs
but in no way threatening.
Blue tits and finches, preoccupied
with the business in hand,
flit from branch to branch.
So too the iconic robin.
Always a beacon of cheeriness,
always an envoy of optimism.
The blackbirds, champion singers
but not just now,
perch around. Maybe they're bored.

Not so the wren,
darting from spot to spot,
a workaholic.
Finally the good old pigeon.
Respectability follows rarity.
He's condemned by commonality.

No my mood has changed so the tree can stay.
But what's this!!
Having listened to me,
others are demanding the tree be
chopped down,
it's blocking their mood as well.
Oh dear, that means I'll have to start
A 'Save Our Tree' campaign.

Never a minute's peace.

Evergreen Two

During the winter I look across from the
bedroom window at the Evergreen and wonder
what, if anything, is hidden from view?
Wonder if the tree has any secrets?
Wonder if there are any diseases, insects or animals,
living or dead, slumbering or decomposing within.

And not unlike a cerebral shell; dense and thick,
there's a shield against intrusion and restless inquisition.
Nosy Parker probing will be resisted and the unconscious
contained in the dark recesses of time allowed to go
festering on, undisturbed, unexamined.

To outward observation it seems to co-exist well with
the neighbouring leaf shedding trees with their naked
branches and their twigs like veins stretching far out across
the broken, blue, patterned sky. Reflected on the terrain.
These trees are open; have no secrets secreted, cloaked
or cocooned within. What you see is what you get.
For them exposure is natural, comfortable. No need
for probing or analysis.

One thinks the evergreen is more interesting.
Presents more of a challenge
But the leaf shedder affords more chance of a quiet
uncomplicated life.

Animal Traffickers

I wish I could put you in a cage
with no concept of freedom
but to feel entrapment instinctively.
With no concept of depression
but to feel despair instinctively.

I wish I could put you in a cage.
To know timelessness.
To alternate between awareness
and shutting down. Retreating.

I wish I could put you in a cage
To pace in sequence endlessly.
To rock back and forth endlessly.
To circle endlessly.
To feel confinement endlessly.

MISCELLANEOUS

Alarming Thought:

"Imagine if, after we died, we found out Shakespeare didn't write any of it!"

February Morning

Lying in bed, looking out the window at
panoramic dismal sheets of rain; wind blown,
sweeping irresistibly, predictably, past layers of
protective double glazing. Thank God!

The tennis has long since drizzled out on
winter soaked courts and there are no custodians
to be seen raking, scarifying or tidying.
No brave dog walkers, usually in evidence
and no shapely lycra filled bottoms to warm
and comfort old lecherous eyeballs.
Nothing!

The evergreens still there of course
bigger than ever but no birds sheltering and
no squirrels following well pattered routes
over well swayed branches.

And yet
There is sanctuary. There is comfort in continuity.
The bleakness. The temporary shutting down.
Boarding up.
There is a cosy hibernation waiting for warmth
and sunshine and spring.

It's a good day to watch an old film with
Alistair Sim and Joyce Grenville.
Or maybe write something
Maybe write a poem

Maybe this poem?

An Original Idea

She said: I've got an original idea!
He said: Oh good. What's that?
She said: What about someone putting on a Shakespeare play wearing sixteenth century costumes?
He said: Well yes, that is a novel idea but only a slim chance I think.
She said: You think so?
He said: Yes. Whistling in the dark I'm afraid Combat and Gastapo uniforms, skin heads, flappers. Anything but traditional. All done and dusted I'm afraid!
She said: Um, I suppose so. Just a thought.

After the Show

He said: Did you enjoy the show?
She said: Yes I did
He said: But you didn't woop, holler and shout at the end.
She said: No I didn't
He said: You only clapped. Why's that?
She said: Because I thought it was good but not that good.
He said: But you still have to woop, holler and shout. It's what people do. Often during the show as well.
She said: You don't think that's at bit Over The Top?
He said: No of course not. (slight pause) You didn't stand up either?

August 3rd 1914

On a bright, warm bank holiday Monday while
German calverymen stared at the Belgium frontier
Jack Hobbs scored 226 at the Oval.
Surrey versus Nottingham. He batted all day.
His highest score to date and a wonderful,
masterful innings, embracing perfection.
So they said.

Of course, the German cavalrymen couldn't see Jack
but fifteen thousand Englishmen did and they cheered
and laughed and waved their hats in the sunshine and
then went on to Whitehall and the Mall where they
cheered and laughed and waved their hats in the sky
and then cheered themselves onto the boats
and cheered themselves into the trenches
and cheered their way onto bullets and bayonets and
soon recorded their own short, ignominious,
stay at the crease.

One wonders
Of the fifteen thousand how many saw Jack again
or how many cherished that memory, in mud and pain,
of a great innings played at the oval, in the sunshine,
before the veil descended and
they batted and cheered their way into eternity.

Note: War was declared on August 4th.

The Chosen

And it came to pass that there was great wailing
and gnashing of teeth across the land.
'Remainers wanted to stay joined with the great
continent across the sea to the east while
'Leavers', fearing only pestilence and the contagion
and spread of barbarians, wanted to leave.

The Lord was greatly displeased with the ungodly ways
of his people and said:
"Now there must be an election and as a punishment
both prophets contesting will be 'unelectable'.

But the people were greatly confused and agitated
and said:
"Lord how is it possible we can elect such an
unelectable prophet? Give us a sign. Show us the way."
But the Lord said:
"You must search the highways and byways of your mind
to select the 'least unelectable'.
That is your punishment."

And so it came to pass across the land,
that after great trials and tribulations
and much wandering of the highways and byways,
especially in the northern climes, that the
'least unelectable' prophet was duly elected.

And some of the multitude rejoiced and feasted
Especially those who kept great wealth and riches
in far off lands and the owners of many houses.
Now they could now sleep soundly in their beds.
Free and untroubled.

But others still wailed and roamed the land
searching for comfort and searching for a new
'unelectable' prophet to show them the way.
So that now it was the Lord's turn to be confused
and agitated and he despaired of his people.
And decided, in future, to stay out of it.

Election 2019

Fate

Sometimes it seems
all the pieces are in place
to ensure survival
and other times in place
to ensure destruction

Underhand Tactics

For me
The computer lies in wait
Waits with underhand tactics
Waits to spring surprises
Lays traps for the unwary
To stumble and fumble and tumble into.

'Sorry we can't open this page'
'Can you verify your pin?'
'Can you enter your password?'
'The network cannot gain access'
'Failure for sending emails'
'Failure for receiving emails'
'Try again later'

For my wife.
Accounts are settled. Prices compared.
Emails received. Emails answered.
Buying on line. Selling on line.
Banking on line.
A friendly computer
All done and dusted
Smooth as clockwork

So
It could be incompetence on my part.
But I think it knows!
Knows when I'm using it.
Lies in wait
Waits with underhand tactics.

The Clock

Tick Tock
Said the clock
Watching us living, seeing us striving
Trying to navigate
Paths ever winding
Tick Tock
Tick Tock
The option of instinct
The option of planning
The option of looking or seeing or scanning.

Tick Tock
Said the clock
Hearing us laughing, hearing us crying
Sometimes we're honest, sometimes we're lying
Tick Tock
Tick Tock
The option of searching
For happiness pining
For love ever lasting
For love never hiding.

Tick Tock
Said the clock.
Seeing us ageing, watching us sliding
Seeing us creaking, watching us dying,
Tick Tock
Tick Tock
Now there are babies snug in their cot's
Soon they'll be growing, soon they'll be striving
Soon they'll be laughing, soon they'll be crying
Soon there are options just as before

Tick Tock
Tick Tock
The clock sees it all
The clock on the wall.

- In the poetry room a loud clock and a challenge to write a poem about a clock -

A Fantasy

Sometimes,
after reading a great poet,
one fantasises being a great poet.
Not always, not often, just sometimes.

And in moments of semi consciousness
to find, drifting in the void, a Golden Dictionary.
And to search for and find, in that dictionary,
rich words, spilling out, collected, harvested.
Then to mould the words into patterns and images,
to launch them into streams of meaning.
To become a precious fabric, used and enjoyed,
worn and displayed, for generations to come.

The slim chance of realisation is sad
and the only comforting thought,
albeit the equivalent of eating gruel,
is that with most great poets,
there aren't many laughs.

Drying Up

In sympathy with the climate
my writing seems to have dried up;
soaked up, seeped away, evaporated.
So perhaps the time has come to
listen to the voices of inevitability
and drift slowly; slowly but surely,
layer by layer, into the giant, waiting,
sticky, gooey, pudding of sloth.
Just to slide away further and further,
deeper and deeper and bit by bit let
folds of inactivity collect around me;
to envelope me in comfortable,
blessed ignorance and BLISS

But HARK!!
In the distance, is that the trumpet
of hope?

Is that the trumpet of possibility?
Is it trying to disturb my ignorance?
Is its sound probing and piercing my pudding?
Push, push, pushing through my pudding,
layer by layer, bit by bit until it finds me.
Then to pull and pull and pull me
upward into the world of trouble,
of news, injustice and emails
to battle away once more.

Good while it lasted?
Well the pudding was comfortable
albeit a tad boring.

The Train

I'm waiting for a train that I hope is delayed.
Hoping it's still some way down the track or
maybe stuck in a siding somewhere.
For me the further away the better.

It's not the daily variety that trundles around locally.
That's the slow train and it stops at all the daily routines
but it's full of things to do so most of the time I like it.
It's a time filling train.
Everyone tries to catch it but some fill its time more
than others. I try to occupy as much as I can
and I'm hoping to stay on it a bit longer.

Of course the big train will arrive one day, one hour,
one minute, one second, one millisecond.
Most people try to avoid it. Pretend it's not coming.
They're really afraid of the uncertain destination.
Others are more confident and believe they
know the final station. Know journey's end.

Either way in the end we're all on board.
There's no more time to fill.
No 'points failures'
or
'leaves on the line'.

In Praise of Short Poems

One Advises

When looking at poems
proceed with great caution.
Consider the size and amount
of each portion.

So try this and that
and like Tapas one feels,
just dip in and out
and avoid heavy meals.

There's plenty on offer,
there's so much to choose.
So get carried away
you've nothing to loose.

There are dishes you know,
some tried before
but then there are new one's
and soon there are more.

You'll find some that are sour
and some that are sweet
and some that are spicy
watch out for the heat.

So when looking at poems
consider congestion.
Don't go for the big ones,
avoid indigestion.

Hidden Depths or Not

The image people project,
consciously or unconsciously,
can be deceptive.
And deviations from that image,
deliberately or accidentally,
can be uncomfortable.

After reading one of my books
a friend of long standing looked
at me pointedly and said:
"I can't believe you wrote this."

The possible implication was that
I had deviated somewhat from his long
held image of an amiable old duffer
not over endowed with cerebral matter
or alternatively had confirmed
with a few taps on the computer
all his preconceptions by producing
such a load of old rubbish.

Now, with poking around and sifting
through musty memory banks, one
recalls his image being altered with the
discovery that he once worked for MI5.
Not to be replaced by a dashing projection
of James Bond but certainly modified a tad.

A World for the Savvy

She said: It's lucky for you I'm around.
He said: In what way?
She said: Managing the finances.
He said: For example?
She said: Surfing the net to look for the cheapest utility prices. The cheapest car insurance, house insurance. Buying on line. Bargaining on the phone. Where to invest. Interest rates. The bond market!
He said: I take the point. The days when prices were the same or similar for everyone are almost gone.
She said: That's right it's competition and knowledge nowadays. You have to be competitive and savvy to survive.
He said: So! Not so good for the less savvy and most of the elderly or the disinterested!
She said: No, it's not. What if I go first? What will you do then?
He said: Look for somewhere else to live I suppose. There must be a more backward planet somewhere in the solar system.

The Storm

October 2021

I'm listening to a storm this morning,
beating remorselessly on the perspex roof,
beating hard, beating rhythmically, a Kalashnikov storm,
a rat-a-tat-tat storm.
And one muses now that storms seem to be everywhere,
covering this land, covering other lands, towns, cities,
continents, everywhere.

Some storms will pass quickly, others are more obdurate
and others still so stubborn, so entrenched they seem
endless. Stretching on and on into the distance, into the
future and beyond the time of many. Beyond the origins
and memories of many.

So what's to do?
Wait patiently or not so patiently?
Stay removed or not so removed?

To stay calm and wait, wait for the threat to pass,
for the threat to recede, to retreat and for warmth
to penetrate, saturate and content the land once more.

Or to have a strategy, to build defences, to challenge the
problems.
And if there must be a strategy to deal with these storms,
it must be an everyone strategy, an everywhere strategy,
we have no choice.

Covid Poems After August 2020

"Sometimes change moves slowly,
sometimes quickly,
and sometimes fundamentally."

Scary

Interesting how, as time passes,
scary can become less scary.
On the beach of covid news, statistics wash up
about Swale, about Thanet, about Maidstone
and somehow they should be scary
but somehow they aren't so scary.
So perhaps as time passes
even plagues can slide into routine.

8/12/2020

Nothing Day

A nothing day today.
Sheets of uninterrupted drizzle,
penetrating, soaking.
A dull, grey, nothing day.
A day to gaze at the sky.
A day to look at a tree.

For others
It's a something day
For 744 people
it's a something day.
Their last day.

23/12/2020

Down on the Coast Two

So now the cloud hangs over us.
No more safety with distance
No more detached spectator

Now we can see,
peering from our hobbit hole's,
people we know, people we knew,
old friends, new friends, people down
the street, people round the corner,
people, people, people,
collected, rounded up, recorded,

And we can say:
Did you know about?
Did you hear about?
Has anyone mentioned?
Only last month he was ...
Only last week she said ...
Only yesterday …

Hundreds died on the last day
before the eleventh hour
before the end of the Great War.

So now...
With foresight.
With knowledge.
With speed.

Lets get the jab
before the cloud gets us.

18/1/2021 - The original 'Down on the Coast' can be found in *Somefink in Particular*, p23 -

Pandemic Tummy

She said: I've noticed that during the pandemic you seem
to have put on weight!
He said: Actually my weight's still the same as it's been for
years! It's just that an important component part
has moved south.
She said: Well, you'll just have to make it go back to where it
came from!
He said: Easier said than done I'm afraid. Now it's settled in
its new surroundings it might not be very
responsive to change. I think it would resist any
attempt at re-location.

5/1/2021

Following the Rules

I heard you drove over to west Kent to
walk with your friend in Tunbridge Wells?
That's right.
Seems a long way to go in the present
circumstances. Aren't we supposed to stay local?
Yes well, Kent is our 'local' county isn't it? I didn't
drive into Sussex.
I see. And then, on the way home, you stopped
off to see your daughter and her family in Ashford?
Yes that's right. They're in my 'bubble'.
And the next day you went to see your aunt
in Folkestone?
That's correct. She lives on her own and I'm in
her 'bubble'. It's all perfectly straightforward.

20/1/2021

The Strategy

The word from some people is
don't watch, don't listen, avoid
information.
Batten down the hatches,
weigh the anchor,
stay safe, stay sure, stay put
below decks

Avoid all the sadness.
Avoid all the layers and layers of sadness.
Emerge only later...
When the sun shines.
When the storm passes.
When the land is warm.
When the birds are singing.

But for now
The storm still rages,
waves crash against the side.
Information's trying to seep in.
And there are leaks, fissures, gaps,
And we know.

And perhaps we should know
we're part of the whole,
part of the struggle.
And perhaps we can show empathy

Captain Tom certainly did
and much, much more.

28/1/2021

A Pandemic Observation

She said: With all this lockdown I think their marriage is
heading for the rocks.
He said: Really, what makes you say that?
She said: Not enough diversions. I've noticed they're
spending more and more time in each others
company and relying on conversation.

The Vaccine

Watching, through the window, at the snow
settling slowly on an encrusted, shivering,
acquiescent garden,

I think of the vaccine in my body, settling down,
taking root, gradually becoming familiar with
arteries, valves, organs; with all the little
nooks and crannies, hidden and obvious.
Travelling to find paths, looking for passageways,
building defenses, making secure.

Eastern religions deify rivers, the river Ganges,
a sacred gift from heaven to flow through valleys,
pastures, towns, cities and to purify, to cleanse,
protect the faithful, bestow salvation.

The source, the origins, the raison d'etre are
different but the objectives, one muses, are
more or less the same.

8/2/2021

Mr Covid

He's a slippery, nasty little customer is Mr Covid
and he knows we're after him
knows we're in pursuit
knows he's on the run
knows he must keep one step ahead.

But at the same time he's bold
not really hiding
not keeping to the shadows.
He's up front and cocky.
Cocky as a rooster.
"You won't catch me,"
he proudly boasts.

And he's a 'master of disguise'.
Travelling incognito.
Changing appearance constantly.
Always on the move,
moving to pastures new.
"You won't catch me,"
he proudly boasts.

Our experts are on his trail.
Could be Sherlock,
Could be Hercule.
Could be both
and they may clip his wings
may slow him up.

But, get rid of him?

He's a slippery customer is Mr Covid.

7/3/21

Spring

Everything's waking up
The bulbs, the shrubs, the trees
Looking for life, searching for life.
Reaching up for the sun,
Straining up for the sun
To give warmth.

For the earth to give warmth,
For the earth to give life.
For hibernation to end
For winter to pass.

And so it is for us
For the cold, covid winter to pass
For the virus to pass.
For death to pass
For life to start again
For life to begin afresh.

Blossom forms on the trees
Blossom falls from the trees
And there's life
Life to nourish
Life to enjoy
Life to consume.

19/3/21

Epilogue

This book is dedicated to the memory
of my sister Davina who died on Christmas day
2017 but also to mention and remember dear
friends Dennis Bryant, Pat Lewis, Peter Reilly
and Les Preston who all died in 2021.

Poets and philosophers acknowledged and quoted, on pages: 35, 48, 52 & 66,
are available within the public domain.
Taken from *Nuffink in Particular Part One:* Old Holiday Photos p6 &
The Evergreen p92 .
Taken from *Nuffink in Particular Part Two:* A Word for the Savvy p109.

Printed in Great Britain
by Amazon

77252212R00082